A Turkey's Thanksgiving Story

Copyright © 2022 Justin Boyd
All rights reserved
First Edition

PAGE PUBLISHING
Conneaut Lake, PA

First originally published by Page Publishing 2022

ISBN 978-1-6624-4393-0 (pbk)
ISBN 978-1-6624-4409-8 (hc)
ISBN 978-1-6624-4394-7 (digital)

Printed in the United States of America

A Turkey's Thanksgiving Story

Written and Illustrated by

JUSTIN BOYD

Every year it always starts out the same. Farmer Fred gets a turkey in July. That turkey spends the next four months getting fattened up to be the guest of honor at the Thanksgiving dinner. This year, the latest victim, or guest, is a turkey named Tom, Tom Turkey.

Tom showed up in a crate the same way all the turkeys before him had. But Tom was special, only he did not know it yet. Tom would change the farm forever.

The first on the farm to greet Tom was a feisty red fighting rooster named Roy Rooster. Roy was very quick to befriend Tom. Roy also explained how life on the farm worked. He explained to Tom that there were two feuding factions or groups on the farm. The chickens or clucks, which he belonged to, and the ducks or quackers, with whom they were feuding.

Roy continued that it was he who had the important job every day of waking Farmer Fred, and Roy took his job very seriously and was never late. Or the farmer might get angry. He also had the important job of watching over the farmer's other chickens. This was, after all, a chicken farm, and the farmer made his living selling the eggs, and you can't have a chicken farm without chickens.

However, the ducks were useless showboats with their flying and swimming. That was all they did, fly and swim and lie around, getting fed and fat off Wilma, the farmer's wife's good nature. She fed them; she liked to feed them. They were charity cases. And they were not even real farm animals. They were just vacationers, he said, visiting from somewhere, and they stayed here for a few months and then flew off somewhere else. Oh, sure, they came back every year, but they didn't really live here, the tourist. And when they were on the farm, they were unbearable.

The ducks were constantly showing off and bragging about their flying and swimming, and the chickens, who were busy working, did not like it. And the ducks served no real purpose on the farm.

But Roy asked Tom for his help. He asked Tom if he would help him set the ducks back in their places and help him remind them that they served no purpose on the farm. Then Roy explained that if one of them could do what the ducks could do, then the ducks would stop bragging all the time.

So Roy wanted Tom to fly.

As a turkey, he was much more adept to this flying business than any of the chickens were. For starters, he had much bigger wings and he had a much, much bigger tail. Roy pointed out that his tail would be the perfect rudder. At this point, all the hens started coming into the yard and commenting on Tom's size and muscles and spurs. He was in. He felt like he really belonged with the chickens. So when the big day finally came, all the ducks waddled into the courtyard on the pond side of the yard and all the chickens lined up on the coop side of the yard. It was Tom's big moment, and he was nervous. Tom was petrified. He and Roy had climbed up on top of the chicken coop overlooking the courtyard. It didn't look so high from down there looking up, but from up here looking down was an entirely different story.

Roy told Tom, "Everyone is watching. Go ahead." Tom took a deep breath and stepped off the edge of the coop and started flapping with all his might. Just the way Roy had told him. Tom had assumed that nature would take over the rest. And to Tom's delight, he started to lift off the edge of the coop. And then, he felt his weight shift and he started to fall toward the ground. *Fast!* And Tom hit the ground hard with a resounding thud. Loud enough to be heard on the other side of the pond. When Tom finally got up, he noticed that everyone was laughing. Roy Rooster and Don Duck were shaking wings and laughing, together. Tom heard Don say to Roy, "That was the best one yet!"

"Yeah", said Roy. "He believed so much that I almost believed too. He really thought he was going to fly."

Don said, "I can't wait until next year!"

Tom couldn't make sense of what he was seeing or hearing. He thought these two were enemies, but here they were, talking like friends. Then, Roy and Don explained to Tom that this was the big event every year on the farm.

"Every year, we get a new turkey, Tom."

"Yeah," said Don. "And every year, Roy tries to convince him to fly."

"And this helps to keep the peace between the chickens and ducks on the farm for a whole year. This eases the tension on the farm, and everyone gets along for a whole other year. But you were amazing!" said Don.

Most turkeys don't get up to the roof, let alone the edge.

"Yeah," said Roy. "We only had one other turkey that made it to the ledge, but never have we had one that actually jumped!"

"And the look on your face…you were determined, like you actually believed. Wow! You sure are amazing! We will never forget you, Tom."

Tom didn't understand why they were talking about him in the past tense, and he couldn't believe what he was hearing. He thought he was among friends. And the whole time they were just playing him for a fool.

And now, he had no friends and was all alone on the farm, and they were laughing at him. Tom was embarrassed and ashamed.

So he ran off to the barn and climbed back into his crate and hid there. He had just about decided to stay there forever. Then he heard a little voice. It was a soft and sweet voice. It was the voice of Charity Chicken. A young chick and Roy's daughter and one of the only chickens who wasn't present at the flight ceremony. She said she refused to attend those ceremonies because they were just mean. She didn't agree with the idea of using someone else's misfortune or situation to help everyone else to be happy and get along.

She came to check on him and tell him she was sorry for what had happened to him.

She didn't think it was funny, and she wanted him to know that. She thought it was sad. And sadder still because Tom had not learned his true purpose on the farm yet.

And she was not alone.

A young duck was with her, Drake Duck, the son of Don Duck. He said he felt the same way Charity did and they were tired of it and wanted it to stop. They had a plan. But first, they needed to explain something to Tom. The reason everyone said that there was a new turkey every year, and the reason they were talking about Tom in the past tense, was, very soon Tom would be invited to Thanksgiving dinner. Then on Thanksgiving, the farmer would come for him to take him to dinner. And that would be the end of Tom. They said they could understand that he had already had a very traumatic day. After what he had been through with their dads, Roy and Don, they could understand him having trust issues.

To that, Tom said, "How do I know I can trust you?"

Drake simply said, "You don't…but you can."

Tom looked at the two youngsters, and he could see no malice in their eyes, only pity and determination. He knew they were both standing up against their fathers and their flocks for him. He said, "All right, what do we do?"

"Well," Drake said, "you can't fly. We all know that. But Roy did have a point. If you could do something miraculous…not only would it stop everyone from laughing at you, but it could quite possibly save your life too."

"How?" asked Tom, genuinely excited now.

"Well, I heard rumors of some pig a couple of counties away and he really wasn't all that special. Point of fact, I can't think of anything special about him. But if you could do something no other turkey could do, that really would be special. And you really would be some turkey! The farmer would surely not invite you to dinner after that!"

Tom asked, "But what could I do that would be that special?"

Charity and Drake both said in unison, "You could swim."

"What?" Tom scoffed. "Me? Swim? How could I possibly do that?"

Drake said, "You're perfect for it. You're…er…ummm…stuffing would actually help you."

Charity said, "Yes. It will help you float, Tom. You will be more buoyant in the water."

"Yeah, yeah!" Drake said. "Fat floats!" Charity gave Drake a stern look. Drake said, "What? It does—"

Charity said, "Roy was right about your tail being the perfect rudder…only in the water…not the air."

And Drake added, "Your big wings are perfect paddles. And I can teach you the basics."

"I can be a lookout and let you know when the coast is clear to get down to the pond," Charity added. "What have you got to lose?" Charity asked.

To this, Tom replied, "Well, everyone will laugh at me."

"They're already laughing," said Drake, "and this is your one chance to make them stop. And it's your only chance to save your life, Tom. We only have two weeks to teach you to swim before Thanksgiving and you go to dinner. So eat a big breakfast. You need to gain as much weight as possible. The more weight you gain, the more buoyant you'll be in the water."

So Tom started eating double portions at every feeding, which made Farmer Fred very happy.

He could be heard saying things like, "This is going to be a great Thanksgiving! Have you ever seen such a terrific turkey?"

Every morning, Tom went down to the pond for swimming lessons with Drake while Charity kept watch. The first one did not go well at all. Tom was afraid to even get in. Once he finally did, however, he slipped and fell, which caused him to freak out and start flapping and squawking. He was making a big hullabaloo, which was sure to get them caught. Drake just tried to shield his face from the splashing and said very calmly, "Just stand up. Tom, put your feet down." And Tom did. Then he started laughing. And so Drake and Charity started laughing too. And the three of them were laughing together. Not at Tom, but *with* Tom. And that felt different than before. This felt good. And Tom knew that he now had real friends. Tom also noticed that he was starting to get attention in the yard as well. All the hens and chicks in the yard, and even the lady ducks, were commenting on the size of Tom's spurs and his leg muscles. They were saying things like, "Have you ever seen drumsticks like those?"

And Roy Rooster and Don Duck started showing off their feathers and standing taller when he was around, even though it was very obvious to everyone else that Tom was much larger and more impressive than they were.

Roy and Don were both now looking forward to Thanksgiving. Just to be rid of the competition.

But Tom still secretly did his swimming lessons every morning, and no one but Drake and Charity knew about it. After a week, Tom knew he was improving. He could now float and paddle in a general direction, and each day he was getting more and more confident in the water, but he didn't know if this would be enough.

The day before Thanksgiving, Tom was able to do figure eights and swim in circles. Tom could even dive down under the water and resurface back on top.

Drake told him he took to swimming like a duck took to water. Which, coming from a duck, Tom felt was a big compliment.

Charity told him he looked like he had been swimming all his life.

Tom felt free on the water, and he could not wait to show the whole yard.

But what would the farmer say? That was the question that had been plaguing him for weeks. If Farmer Fred was not impressed, then it would all be for nothing.

Charity saw the look of worry on Tom's face. "What's wrong, Tom?"

"Well," said Tom, "what if it doesn't work? What if the farmer still invites me to the Thanksgiving meal? Then all this effort will have been for nothing!"

"No, Tom. Not for nothing. Have you noticed the respect you've been getting in the yard lately?"

"Yeah," said Charity. "Even from Don and Roy."

"Even from the farmer," added Drake. "Everyone has said there has never been a turkey on the farm like you before, Tom. And they are right!"

This made Tom feel a little better. At least until he started walking back up to the roost for the night. Tom saw the farmer sharpening his ax in the shed and heard him whistling to himself happily.

Tom kept hearing that whistling all night long. Tom had dreams of being chased by whistling axes all night long. The next morning, Tom was tired and nervous. Finally, he walked up and announced that he had a Thanksgiving surprise for all of them. The whole yard got quiet, and Tom said, "Today I will do the impossible. Something that up until now…only the ducks could do on the farm."

Roy pushed his way to the front of the crowd, and so did Don. "What have we here?" said Roy.

Don started laughing and said, "We've seen this before."

Roy said, "Yeah…turkeys lose their minds at the thought of being invited to Thanksgiving dinner."

And Don said, "Are you going to try to fly again? With all that extra weight you've gained, when you fall again…at least you'll have a soft landing.

"Soft?" said Roy. "He will probably bounce!"

And the whole yard started to laugh, again.

Tom could feel himself getting embarrassed and flustered, and Roy started strutting up and down and raising his feathers. The hens started to all gather around him.

Then Charity Chicken spoke up. She told them to stop laughing at him. She said, "He has not cracked his egg. He is perfectly sane. And he's right."

"That's right!" Drake piped up. "He's no Humpty-Dumpty! He's my friend, and you all need to stop laughing at him."

The laughter slowed down and died away. There was a look of confusion on all the faces in the yard.

Drake said, "Tom, can do something that, up until now, only the ducks could do? Tom can swim."

The entire yard erupting into peals of laughter.

Charity, squawking at the top of her lungs, said, "That's right. He can. And I've seen it!"

Don calmed everyone down and said, "This wonderful Thanksgiving turkey has decided to give us one more show as a final, parting gift. Let us not be rude. Let's all humor him and go down to the pond."

Roy said, "Don is right. Don, I don't think there will ever be another turkey like this Tom."

So all the chickens and all the ducks gathered around the pond right before the sun came up.

Just as the sun was coming up over the pond and Roy was about to do his morning duty, Tom stepped out of the crowd and into the water.

A hush fell over the crowd. Immediately, Tom started sinking. The ducks started laughing.

The chickens started laughing.

Then they all leaned in closer as Tom sank down beneath the surface.

Don was just about to go into the water to get Tom out when Tom burst out of the water and splashed the whole crowd of laughing ducks and chickens.

This was his plan all along.

Then Tom started doing the most impressive display of swimming ever seen outside of Sea World. The chickens and ducks were standing at the edge of the pond, openmouthed, and the sun was fully up now.

The farmer came out muttering about useless roosters and stood at the edge of the pond and couldn't believe what he saw.

This amazing, swimming turkey.

The farmer was so shocked he dropped his ax and ran into the house, picked up the phone receiver, and dialed a bunch of numbers and said, "Hello, newsroom! Yeah…I've got a story for you. You think that pig was special? Well, I have an exceptional and terrific turkey. He's not only the most impressive turkey I've ever seen, he can swim too! That's right! That's what I said. Yes, he can swim! No, I have not been in the eggnog early. This is most certainly not a publicity stunt. Come and see for yourself. Okay! You'll be here in an hour? I'll see you then."

This is going to really put our little farm on the map, he thought.

"Wilma, honey, there's a change of plans. We're not having turkey this year. Maybe we will get rid of that useless old red rooster or one of your useless ducks!"

And at hearing this, Roy let out the biggest crow he had ever crowed. Don said, "Well, would you look at those trees? Is it time to migrate already? Where does the time go? My, my, my, how the time flies! And now so do I. See ya!" Then he added, "Come on, flock, let's take flight out of here before we get an invitation to dinner! Let's get the flock out of here!"

With that, Don and the rest of the ducks took off and were last seen flying south. All except Drake, who stayed behind. He figured he was too small for a dinner invitation, and he wanted to see how things turned out for his friend Tom.

But as for Tom, he was not invited to Thanksgiving dinner, after all!

About the Author

Justin Boyd lives in Forney, Texas, with his wife Jennifer, his three children, Noah, Allison, and Brooklyn, and his three stepchildren, Aiden, Isaac, and Eli. He was an elementary classroom teacher for ten years. He received his teaching certification from Texas A&M University, as well as his master's degree in education administration.

He created this story to entertain his own children, who then suggested that he write it down. Then his children said he should turn it into a real book. He wanted to show them that ordinary people can do great things, so he followed the advice of his children, who believed in him, and the manuscript was selected to become a real book. His children wanted him to follow his dreams like he always taught them to follow their dreams.

He hopes that all the children who read the book enjoy it as much as his own children did, and hopes they remember that impossible things can happen if they just believe.

CPSIA information can be obtained
at www.ICGtesting.com
Printed in the USA
BVHW060135191122
652284BV00003B/19